REACHING FOR THE SUN

REACHING FOR THE SUN

Meditations

ANGELA HERRERA

SKINNER HOUSE BOOKS
BOSTON

Copyright © 2012 by Angela Herrera. All rights reserved. Published by Skinner House Books, an imprint of the Unitarian Universalist Association of Congregations, a liberal religious organization with more than 1,000 congregations in the U.S. and Canada, 25 Beacon St., Boston, MA 02108-2800.

www.skinnerhouse.org

Printed in the United States

Cover design by Kathryn Sky-Peck
Text design by Suzanne Morgan

print ISBN: 978-1-55896-665-9
eBook ISBN: 978-1-55896-666-6

6 5 4 3 2 1
15 14 13 12

Library of Congress Cataloging-in-Publication Data

Herrera, Angela.
  Reaching for the sun : meditations / Angela Herrera.
    p. cm.
  ISBN 978-1-55896-665-9 (pbk. : alk. paper)—ISBN 978-1-55896-666-6 (ebook)
 1. Meditations. 2. Unitarian Universalist Association. I. Title.
 BV4832.3.H48 2012
 242—dc23
                                        2011051373

For Carlos—my co-adventurer, my love.

With gratitude to David—
dear friend, applier of red ink.

CONTENTS

Introduction	ix
Invocation	1
Courage	2
A Laying-On of Words	4
In the Garden	5
I Use What I Have	6
Alder Street	8
How It Is	10
Living It Up	12
In the Church Food Pantry Line	13
One Good Anger	14
Loving Is Dangerous	15
The Student Chaplain Goes On Call	16
All I Could Say Was Amen	18
Hear Our Prayers	20
Sometimes It Takes a Little Craziness	21
Lucky Streak	23
The Bath	24
Sometimes When We Pray	26

Utterance of the Timeless Word	28
Love and Ficuses	30
Beneath the Hustle and Bustle	32
Grief	34
Uncounted Psalm	36
All of Us in the Arms	37
Doubting Thomas	38
Prayer for Travelers	40
Oración para los Viajeros	42
All That You Need Lies Within You	44
How Poets Pray	46
Unitarian Universalist Meditation Manuals	47

INTRODUCTION

The first draft of this meditation manual slid out of my printer on a bright, busy fall day, at the beginning of my second year of ministry.

I skimmed the pages as they landed one on top of another, and recognized my life flashing before my eyes. Here is the small-town trailer park where I grew up with a scrappy cohort of friends, running barefoot and getting into mischief. Here is my adolescence, and my mother struggling to propel us out of poverty by earning her high school diploma and then going to college. Here I am becoming a mother myself, too soon, at the age of nineteen.

The piece called "Grief" slides onto the pile, and I remember my daughter's birth. The poem recalls the painful separation of mother and baby—first through labor and then as the child becomes an adult—and links me with a stranger half a world away. But the year my daughter was born was marked by other kinds of grief: postpartum depression and a profound sense of failing to live up to my potential. That pain would become a source of strength and insight later, but at the time it brought me to my knees and kindled my anger.

Back then, my husband and I were very young, unskilled, and on public assistance. From the outside, things did not seem promising. In the grocery store and at the library, at the doctor's office and at the park, I received rude comments and condescending looks. Indignant, I glared back. I wanted to be taken seriously.

My mother taught me to love outrageous dreams. One day, as I nursed my infant daughter in the living room of our tiny, sparsely furnished apartment, an impossible thought popped into my head: by the time she is ten years old, I will have a master's degree from Harvard. The idea was so far-fetched that I tucked it away in the back of my mind and nearly forgot about it, turning my attention instead to mothering. Over the next five years, my husband and I worked hard and bought a little house. I gave birth to baby number two, a son. The poem "In the Garden" takes place in our backyard, where the kids plucked fresh peas and beans off the vines, hunted insects, and played as I contemplated our life together.

During that time, I wandered into the Unitarian Universalist Congregation of Salem, Oregon. When I was a child, my family often attended a UU church in Portland, but I drifted away when I became embarrassed by the contrast between our social class and that of my Sunday school peers. Now, returning to the faith as a young adult, I found a community of welcoming elders. They took me under their wings, inviting me to work alongside them in virtually every function of the church, from serving coffee to serving on the board of directors. Our minister, Rick

Davis, guided me as I found my feet, first as an adult and then as a developing leader. I enrolled in community college and began to imagine what I might do with the rest of my life.

One day, on the way home from school, I realized I would become a minister. It came out of the blue—one minute I had never thought of it before, and the next it was unavoidable, even though it was terrifying and I figured everyone would tell me I was nuts. I said it out loud to a few people at church to see if they'd laugh and I'd be off the hook. But instead they encouraged me. I went to the Unitarian Universalist Association website, and looked up the path to ordination. A full page of requirements, each with multiple sub-steps, appeared before me. At the top of the list was earning a Master of Divinity degree. At that time, only a few schools were listed as preferable for UU students. Among them was Harvard.

What happened next feels like a blur in hindsight. The doors flew open. Good grades and volunteer work at church helped me win a full scholarship for my bachelor's degree in Oregon, with an option to reapply for graduate funding anywhere in the country. Two of my professors—both Harvard alumni—offered to write letters of recommendation. My husband and I put plane tickets on the credit card, and traveled to Boston for Harvard's prospective student day. I wandered the campus in disbelief and returned home filled with anguish over how much I yearned to study there, and what a long shot it still was. Then in the spring of 2005, the impossible happened: I received both the graduate scholarship and an acceptance letter to Harvard. My daughter was nine years old.

I share this story because all theology is ultimately autobiographical. Entire religious traditions develop from the seeds of individual experience and the timeless, intimate question: *What does this mean?* This collection of meditations draws from my lived experience on the winding path from the gritty neighborhood of my childhood, to marriage and motherhood, to the Ivy League, and then to my first pastorate in Albuquerque, New Mexico. It includes themes of longing, brokenness, and love; of idealism, vulnerability, and fear; of coming up short and—most especially—of redemption. It takes courage and a leap of faith to follow the soul's calling, but we humans are frail. Our courage and faith are prone to faltering.

"Uncounted Psalm" is a lament in the style of our religious ancestors, who bore testament to the way all these themes crash together in the real-world lives of God's children. We are no less beloved, no less inherently worthy or dignified, for our shortcomings. Rather, it is only through our foibles and flaws, our questioning, striving, and awe, that we may find the sacred in "the mess and the mystery" of life, as my mentor, Gary Smith, would say.

Since theology is autobiographical, it is surely limited. But I hope—I pray—that these meditations are not ultimately about me, for they could only have been formed in relationship with others, and the question *What does this mean?* is universal.

I have met—and continue to meet—a wide variety of people, from gang members and prison inmates to distinguished professors and politicians. I have witnessed births and deaths among the outrageously wealthy and the desperately poor. I bless babies, officiate weddings, lay hands on the sick, and lead memorial services. The most striking lesson I've learned is how similar we all are. We all love, we all cry, we all worry, we all doubt ourselves. We are all vulnerable to getting hurt or hurting others. And I have never known anyone who was not in need of redemption.

To be human is to be both free and limited, and we all bumble around in that paradox, trying to carve out lives with order, love, and meaning. We stumble a lot. Sometimes we trip over our own feet and fall flat. But if we are lucky, we also experience wonder that a world with so much wrongdoing, misfortune, and heartbreak is also marked by undefeatable love, rebirth, and connection.

The last of the meditations slip from the printer onto the desk. How quickly the pages pile up, years compressed between them. They demonstrate another universal truth: the passing of time. Luckily, it is never too late to find the right path or to discover new and unexpected meaning. Never too late to discover that you are whole and holy and in good company in this world, however particular your private experience.

Whoever you are, wherever you are on your journey, may it be a rich and meaningful adventure.

Blessings to you.

INVOCATION

Don't leave your broken heart at the door;
    bring it to the altar of life.
Don't leave your anger behind;
    it has high standards
    and the world needs vision.
Bring them with you,
    and your joy
    and your passion.
Bring your loving,
    and your courage
    and your conviction.
Bring your need for healing,
    and your power to heal.
There is work to do
    and you have all that you need to do it
    right here in this room.

COURAGE

Sometimes it hits you all at once,
what people are capable of—
the hardness of the human heart,
our animal desire for instant reward,
our knack for justification.

Behold the destruction:
economies in crisis,
environmental doom,
profit over purpose
sparking calls for occupation.

Will the same capacities
save us from ourselves?
How creaturely are the children of God . . .
and how creative.

I look outside, at the city—
not the romantic kind, with
buildings that reach for the divine,
casting shadows on the masses,
monuments to the human spirit.
Mine is a city of gas stations and Minimarts,
drab stores with oversized parking lots,
mediocre businesses with unimaginative signs.

The roads are treeless.
There are mountains—yes. And wide sky,
and light, unmatched, that changes all day long.
But today I inhabit the lower places
because we need courage,
and it was gutsy,
building a Walmart
on God's beautiful earth.

A LAYING-ON OF WORDS

I know you are wicked busy, but I need a prayer right now. I'm going into emergency surgery, my friend texts. I picture her on the hospital bed with her stomach in knots, casting prayer requests into the 3-G network.

I see the pre-op unit in my mind: rows of beds and blue curtains bent around corners; staff taking vitals, handing out pills, putting in IVs; student chaplains making nervous rounds, having been on-call all night, having seen some of yesterday's pre-ops sipping juice, and having seen some dead. Exactly what use is a prayer?

I text a blessing back: *Love is all around you. I am holding you in my heart.*

And careening through cyberspace, it tumbles together with the blessings sent by her other friends at the exact same moment—all the words weighty with friendship histories and intimate knowing: the loves-hearts-God-protects-safe-prayers-healings. Picture them pouring into her hospital room, sparkling through the air, landing all over her: a laying-on of words.

See her brow un-knit and peace sweep through her body. A prayer is love in motion.

IN THE GARDEN

We love worms,
the kids and I.
We watch the disgusting things
blindly navigate the soil,
swimming in our ancestors,
feeding each generation
with nutrients from the last.

My vegetables soak it up,
reaching for the sun
like my children,
who get taller
every year,
only to return
to the dirt someday
along with their mother.

My heart breaks,
but swells,
with this notion of our time together
temporary
and infinite.

I USE WHAT I HAVE

I ran this morning
surpassing a personal best.
Past the bakery,
with each inhalation I tasted
pastries, a cigarette, and coffee with fat.
I passed the firehouse and its
strapping young things.
Ran up the hill, thinking
get there, get there.
Winked at the biker dude
who thinks I run for him.
Chasing my six foot
shadow toward noon.

Arriving home in a sweat,
heart racing,
I give thanks.

There are limits to this body—
under five feet tall
with shoes on,
having borne two children,
and being nearly forty.
It's too late for break dancing.
My love sets wine glasses out of reach
and I have to get a chair.
I take pills

and use an inhaler.
The list gets longer every year.

But what exhilaration
to use what you have
and do what you can.
To push it to the limit
so you have to catch your breath.
Good advice for bodies,
and for life.

ALDER STREET

Last week I went to my hometown
and saw the impoverished street
where I once lived,
its flimsy shacks, and dirty children
making late-night runs
for tadpoles in the flooded ditches
that border all the yards.

From the mansion on the hill
(which is just a bungalow)
to the street with the houses
of the upper lower class,
they dip their stolen Tupperware
in runoff from the orchard,
watch out for broken bottles,
or the tadpoles get dissected.

The row of mobile homes
has withstood the yearly windstorms
blowing off the siding.
True to form, the owners curse and,
smoking,
nail them back up.

Slugs still make their way
between the carpet and the dry rot.
Angry footsteps run the risk of
crashing through onto the gravel.

The sun set, inconspicuous,
as dads arrived from mill-work.
The Mormons with their Bibles
make the day's best entertainment.
On bicycles, with neckties,
they proclaim their burning bushes.
It clashes with the beer and guns,
so poor folks bar the door.

HOW IT IS

When the singing bowl signals the end of meditation
inevitably
my mind has just come back.
Not from deep stillness
or enlightenment,
but from its repetitive wanderings
into trifles.
So that after I've daydreamed about
    telling someone off
    or going somewhere else
    or losing someone close

    God help me

Just when I've caught myself and
gently guided my mind back to focus—
    Ding.
It's over and I think, *Again!*
I missed it again.
Then the piano picks up
and the church people gently come
forward to light their candles.

The other day
I closed my eyes as the people rose,
heard the creak of pews and
movement down the aisles,
sensed the heat of a quiet crowd

passing near me like a great migration,
their sweeping and shuffling toward the candles
each person carrying a private burden.
Some of these the minister knows.
Watching from the pulpit, she knows
which flames are lit by those consumed with
the same diagnosis
    or misfortune
the same self-hatred
    or need for forgiveness
    or prayer for improvement.
There is nothing new under the sun and she wishes
   she could
tell the people
how much they have in common
    how human they are
    how beloved they are
each one a child of the holy source.

In truth
I'm not very poetic.
Metaphors don't come easily to me.
I'm just telling you how it is:
the trifles
and the movement
and the burning light.

LIVING IT UP

They take advantage of us, he said. I worked forty years in a factory. Paid taxes. Followed the law. Why should they be living it up on welfare, food stamps?

I thought of the woman with the thick, dark hair, and the nine-months pregnant belly. *No voy al hospital*, she said. Undocumented. Uninsured.

I translated for the midwives but there wasn't much to say. She labored quietly on the bedspread, biting down on a rag. As the baby crowned, I noticed mold growing up the wall, spreading out from the window, moist and dark and poisonous. The curtains sagged around it and rested on the matted brown carpet. She wouldn't report it to the landlord. Didn't want to make trouble.

¡Lo hiciste! I told her, when he was born. You had your baby! But she greeted him solemnly. He gazed at her with shining eyes, face made for his mother's milk.

Living it up? The factory worker had some other image in mind, I guess. I don't blame him. They were the most invisible people I had ever met.

IN THE CHURCH FOOD PANTRY LINE

The day before Thanksgiving:
a woman in a beautiful beaded dress
a man with no teeth
a young man with a pierced lip
and one in his forties,
covered in tattoos.
Several young mothers,
a crowd of little girls,
boys flipping and turning on a rail,
and hopping up our sanctuary steps.

Our steps,

but *their* steps as well, if we mean it,
    this inherent worth and dignity;
and if there's an interdependent web
    and we didn't just make that up;

their steps, if we get radical
    and believe that love is justice,
and welcome people in.
Theirs if we overcome our fear
that we'll be overwhelmed by need.

What's ours is theirs,

fifteen children
and seventy adults,
the day before Thanksgiving
on the sanctuary steps.

ONE GOOD ANGER

Some traditions teach calm, equanimity. All is illusion, the Buddhists say. But I don't feel like taking a breath. Sometimes you want to be mad. Even God rages in the ancient texts. Zeus threw lightening bolts. Lilith spawned her demon children. And look at Mother Kali, wearing her string of severed heads.

"You can get a whole house cleaned up on one good anger," my mother says. (I tease her: And the dishes flying? You sure cleaned out the cupboards.)

But I remember after the divorce, how she stormed and cleared the way. Hauled us out of the trailer park and pitched us toward the future. She wouldn't let it go. My sister went to law school. I ended up at Harvard.

There are some people you don't want to cross. But there are others who, angered, will light the night sky.

LOVING IS DANGEROUS

Coughing and gagging
in a teary-eyed, late-night
hour of need,
my daughter reminds me
I'm weak,
powerless to keep
the world in check
or bellicose bacteria from igniting
total war in a body composed of
such skinny arms
and so much roundness.

Sleeping behind me: my son,
the other part of my heart,
brought forth to skip backwards
wanting of protective gear—
what stunts he executes!
Poets know loving is dangerous.
I was warned going in
but I stormed the gates
with abandon,
winged to the flame
like a mystic.

THE STUDENT CHAPLAIN GOES ON CALL

Three deaths.

The first man slouched atwist in bed,
young wife pressed to his side.
She leaned in near his head,
whispered blessings,   wailed, sobbed
in her family's sixteen arms,
their tears collecting on the tiles.
I prayed,
cried inside,
and blessed their loss.

The next arrived dead.
Airway taped and tubed, yet
blankets over his body
hid his still face from view.
His striking son
wept
inarticulate from shock.
My fingers tested,
rested,
in his twisting black hair,
blessed
as I read the prayer,
a psalm,
for the second time.

Dawn had still not broken
when the pager beeped again.
An old woman,
mother, wife,
in a circle of quiet Catholics,
her breaths seizing
the dark night.
A weathered old man at her side
muttered fifty-six years,
married fifty-six years.
My cool hands touched her crown,
helpless. Blessing,
here's a psalm.

ALL I COULD SAY WAS AMEN

I went on a silent retreat.
Sitting with a steaming tea cup
I watched a cardinal outside
in an azalea thicket.   He twitched
    hopped
from tangle   to tangle of branches
and flew   into the glass.
    Bap
against the silence in the house.
    Bap
again, darting as if to come to the table.
    Bap
ten times in all. Then left.

I went outside.
Past the steps,
then down a pebbled road, I entered the New
    England woods

and it was autumn.
I trod where cardinals go
unimpeded
under a steady rainfall of leaves from
the intricate ceiling.

I walked the kneeling hills that
bowed beneath the heavens like
prostrated believers,

thrusting their leaves into
the gray electric sky.

All I could say was Amen.

Sometimes God is flighty
as the songbird.
And sometimes God seeps in
with the steady rain.

HEAR OUR PRAYERS

O God, we pray, not to request your presence, but to call ourselves into it, for the sustaining peace, the wisdom, the silence are nearer than breath. You are the ground of being, the mover, the fire, and the place of rest.

O Love, hear our prayers:

> For the wounded, may there be comfort.
> Let the weary be held in your hands,
> May the joy of the thankful be overflowing,
> Let none be lonely in our community,
> And may we tread gently upon this earth.

SOMETIMES IT TAKES A LITTLE CRAZINESS

When you arrive at the store and can't remember why,

and you forget the vet appointment and almost miss the dentist, even though they called you yesterday,

and the bills are late and your kids need homework help and you are behind at work and haven't exercised in weeks,

and you've been eating fast food while vegetables wilt in your fridge and your garden is turning into compost and the one time you try to cook you leave the granola in the toaster oven, setting the damn thing on fire,

and you double book yourself again and laundry forms mountains around your home and you begin to look askance at your beloved because you haven't had fun together since you can't remember when,

and then, just as you are starting to wonder about signs of dementia, you find yourself placing a metal spoon in the microwave and turning it on . . .

just breathe.

Sometimes it takes a little craziness to get your attention.

The prophet Elijah fled from a hundred pursuers. He hunkered down in a cave on the wind-whipped mountainside, trembled through an earthquake, and shielded his face from a wildfire. He looked for God in the chaos. But when the storms blew over, when the shaking stilled and the flames died down, he crouched, panting, and thinking he'd missed it, his heart pounding in his ears. Then he finally noticed the still small voice.

The holy waits in your world, too. Maybe today it will find you in a listening posture, and will whisper to you.

"You tumble like a leaf," it will say. "And yet by some miracle you are still here. Now what is the purpose of that?"

LUCKY STREAK

Who cast a spell over my world?
Who opened the doors,
stirred the crowd of possibilities,
put gold dust in my dreams
causing my life to turn?

O Fate, O Love, O Spirit, O God:
is it true
that all good things must end?

Or have you set me on a path of meaning
    Not luck
Of clarity
    Not magic

And this grace
that brought me to the mountaintop
is also assigned to carry me through dark forests of
    loss,
    the ones that await us all,
    that disturb our peaceful sleep.

The same grace that guides the seasons:
cracking the ice,
pushing up saplings,
scattering the earth with their first dramatic leaves.

THE BATH

This is what one hundred years look like:
A rounded wrinkled back,
sparkling wet and soapy above the shower bench,
and my hand,
having gently formed in your seventieth year,
and emerged with lifelines bent toward blessing,
scrubbing circles across your soft, white skin.

I drag the cloth beneath your arms,
silently blessing each bend and crease
of breasts and belly, whose curves were determined
in the womb
of my great-great
grandmother.

When you are dry and warm,
one hundred mantras of gratitude
sweep over my heart
that I am the one standing in the frosted light,
rubbing wisps of fragrant talcum into each sweet
    fold.

Tomorrow I return to Boston,
and you'll keep on in your chair
by the picture window
looking down at Seattle.
You are too old to tell your stories now
and have all but ceased speaking,

your thank you honeys
like gems at a silent retreat.

But the stories have become me,
the lifelines that led to my lifelines,
and your name was mine
long before I was dreamed
and was born.

For now there's no reason
to talk.
I adorn you with perfume and color.
Powder, lipstick, rouge.
We get out the pearls.
Looking down at your toenails,
with a fresh coat of glittery red,
you erupt in laughter.

    Will you have to take it off?

All day I kiss you
as often as I can
without making you suspicious
that I'm saying goodbye,
knowing that when you're gone,
I will rise a generation.
And as storylines are lifelines,
I too shall pass them on.

SOMETIMES WHEN WE PRAY

Sometimes when we pray, we bow our heads
Not in subservience, but because it is we, and not our
    neighbor, who need prayer
We bow our heads in search of the silence within,
Or that we might listen, and be comforted,
> We are weak and need strength,
> We are frightened and need courage,
> We are humble and thankful,

And so we bow our heads.

Sometimes we pray with our chins lifted
Facing the heavens,
Receptive, accepting,
Life flowing over and through us,
> We are anxious and need patience,
> We are searching, and need direction,
> We are grateful and radiant,

And so we lift our faces.

And sometimes prayer pours forth in words from
    our lips.
O God, we say,
O Life, O Mystery,

We pray
For all who will be born into this
dangerous and beautiful world today,
and for all who will die.

Love, pour down on them.
May they be safe, and may we,
may they be at peace, and may we,
may they be a blessing upon the world, and may we,
every one.

UTTERANCE OF THE TIMELESS WORD

You bring yourself before the sacred,
before the holy,
before what is ultimate and bigger than your lone
 life
bigger than your worries
bigger than your money problems
bigger than the fight you had with your sister and
 your aches and pains
bigger, even, than your whole being, your self who is
  part of
  and trapped within
  and blessed with
a body that does what you want
and doesn't do what you want
and wants all the wrong things
and wants all the right things . . .

You stand at the edge of mystery,
at the edge of the deep,
with the light streaming at you,
and you can't hide anything—not even from
 yourself,
when you stand there like that,
and then . . . what?

Maybe you call your pastor and say,
  What is this?

    What am I looking at?
    What do I do?
And your pastor comes and stands at the edge with you
and looks over.
She can't hide anything either, she thinks,
not even the fact that she doesn't know the answer to your question,
and she wonders if you can tell.

She thinks of all the generations who've come there before you
and cast words out toward the source of that light,
wanting to name it.
Somehow, she thinks to herself, the names stayed tethered to the aging world and got old
while the light remains timeless and burns without dimming.

    Meanwhile,
the armful of worries you brought to the edge of mystery
have fluttered to your feet.
Unobscured by these, you shine back,
    light emanating unto light.
You, with your broken heart and your seeking,
you are the utterance of the timeless word.
The name of the Holy is pronounced
through your being.

LOVE AND FICUSES

I used to have a ficus.
A beautiful thing, bright
green and leafy,
but once a year
I developed a horrible allergy to it
and became ill.
Once I moved it to a different window
and watched its leaves drop.
Turns out, ficuses—ancestors of the ancient fig—
live in harmony with their environment.
They like consistency of
light, water, air.

Change sends them into a panic.
And ficuses and their owners
may occasionally become enemies.
For a while.

A marriage is like that.

It has good times and bad.
A marriage
bears fruit that will fall, bitter or sweet,
into the hands of loved ones and passers-by.
It takes in light not of its own making,
drinks from the living stream
where it has set down roots.

Dislocate it, disrupt its symbiosis, and
you'll have some work to do.
You'll see what withers and needs removing.
Panic may set in—but don't despair.
Let the leaves fall where they may.
After the dramatic display,
love and ficuses
adapt.

BENEATH THE HUSTLE AND BUSTLE

Beneath the hustle and bustle,
beneath the stream of thoughts
that clambers and chatters
over the landscape of our interior world,
beneath our habits of momentum and stirring,
there is a stillness,
deep and peaceful,
the place where creation begins.

Who lives there?
We know her by many names. Truth. Love. God. Wisdom.
We turn our hearts toward her face,
toward the mystery,
and bring our prayers of awe, of longing, of hope, of exhaustion.

She holds us in our grief and anger,
in our disappointment, our loneliness, and our rebirth.
From her viewpoint she sees us
    Children of the stillness
    Children of love
She sees our place in the order of things
joined together in the larger story
and she invites us again and again into living,

invites us into loving,
invites us into being loved.

May we be restored to wholeness
and blessed with peace.
May all those whom we encounter
receive this blessing
through our being in the world.

GRIEF

The Taliban strapped explosives
to an eight-year-old girl,
and sent her through a checkpoint,
detonating remotely.

I remember the work it took
to bring a daughter into the world;
crying out, bring-you-to-your-knees kind of work.
Two days of tidal birth pains
and the midwives' steady hands upon me.

And how, even now,
as she learns to drive and kiss,
and thinks of college,
my daughter's existence is
an ongoing separation, so that
as she chatters away on the sofa tonight—
her cleavage overflowing a v-neck shirt—
I notice her lips, still rosebud shaped,
and all I can think is how I loved to nurse her.

Grief seizes me so often these days,
the closer she gets to leaving.

Where was that Taliban girl's mother, I wonder.
Her daughter's adolescence would have been so different from mine,
her dreams and chattering a world away,
but our birth pains would have been
the same.

UNCOUNTED PSALM

Why did I listen to Your calling, O God?
Why did I step out on faith, O Love?
Why did I lift my feet,
ignore my fear,
and run toward the unknown?
Now I am far from home.
My heart aches for my familiar land,
for people who greeted me with kisses.
I can't see the way back—it doesn't exist.
I can't see the way forward,
but I long for the place I knew.
By the time I find the way,
my children will be grown and gone.
But today You are silent.
The voice that whispered wind into my sails has stilled.
Fear rises in me like a tsunami far from shore.
Tonight, I will sleep without comfort.

ALL OF US IN THE ARMS

This is a prayer for a fresh, unremarkable morning
a prayer to bring us to attention before the steadiness of the world
>sunrises and sunsets, back and forth
>like the rocking of your grandmother's chair,
>life coming and going, rising and falling,
>droning and beating like ancient music

and you, remarkable for your ordinariness within it,
and your thinking about it, and your yearning for meaning.

You, dependent, spun into the interdependent web,
confined to a body.
You, independent, conscious, free, and so
sometimes also lonely, but unconfined in spirit.
This is a prayer for you, for your well-being, your peace,
your deep peace,
and for everyone you love, and for their well-being,
and for the friends we haven't met yet
and for the strangers we'll never meet,
though we are closer to them than we think,
all of us, in the arms of the earth,
our mother,
with her rocking and singing.

DOUBTING THOMAS

In the Gospel of Thomas, Jesus says, "If you bring forth what is within you, what you bring forth will save you. If you do not bring forth what is within you, what you do not bring forth will destroy you."

Jesus may be right, but the reverse is also true. To bring forth what is within you is to destroy the self that had brought forth nothing.

Picture Jesus cutting wood, the subtle weight of nails in his pocket, his collection of tools. As a carpenter he fashioned tables, ran his hands over their smooth tops. He left that simple work behind for the wilderness, the desert, for the uncertainty of transforming human hearts.

History destroys and remakes him. And every spring, in ritual, he is killed and rises again.

"Follow me," he says. Say goodbye to what you know. Now is the time for transformation.

It's a terrifying order. And so we avoid change—holding what is within us at bay, burying it for the comfort of our routines. This might save us, but only by aborting the person we could have become.

If we would really live, we must be willing to die within the seasons of our lives. Even the path of sameness leads to death by stagnation. The question is: Will you be reborn? Will you press through the darkness and constraint, the danger of your remaking?

And when you do, what will you bring forth?

PRAYER FOR TRAVELERS

This is a prayer for all the travelers.
For the ones who start out in beauty,
who fall from grace,
who step gingerly,
looking for the way back.
And for those who are born into the margins,
who travel from one liminal space to another,
crossing boundaries in search of center.

This is a prayer for the ones whose births
are a passing from darkness to darkness,
who all their lives are drawn toward the light,
and keep moving,
and for those whose journeys
are a winding road that begins
and ends in the same place,
though only when the journey is completed
do they finally know where they are.

For all the travelers, young and old,
aching and joyful,
weary and full of life;
the ones who are here, and the ones who are not here;
the ones who are like you (and they're all like you)
and the ones who are different (for in some ways, we each travel alone).

This is a prayer for traveling mercies,
and surefootedness,
for clear vision,
and bread
for your body and spirit,
and water,
for your safe arrival
and for everyone you see along the way.

ORACIÓN PARA LOS VIAJEROS

Esta oración es para todos los viajeros.
Para los que comienzan en la belleza
y caen de la gracia,
quienes caminan tímidamente,
buscando la manera de volver.
Y para los que nacen en los márgenes,
viajando de un lugar liminal a otro,
cruzando fronteras
en busca del centro.
Es una oración para aquellos cuyo nacimiento
es el paso de oscuridad a oscuridad,
aquellos que se sienten atraídos por la luz,
y avanzan hacia ella.
Y para aquellos cuyas jornadas
son un camino sinuoso
que comienza y termina en el mismo lugar,
aunque sólo al terminar,
sabrán por fin donde están.

Para todos los viajeros,
jóvenes y viejos,
dolientes y alegres,
cansados y llenos de vida;
los presentes y los ausentes,
los que son como tú (y todos son como tú)
y los que son distintos (porque de alguna manera
    todos viajamos solos).

Esta es una oración por la misericordia,
para que andes con pie firme,
y visión clara;
por el pan para tu cuerpo y tu espíritu,
por el agua;
para que llegues seguro,
y para todos aquellos que encuentres
en el camino.

ALL THAT YOU NEED LIES WITHIN YOU

Consider this an invitation
    to you.
Yes—you
with all your happiness
and your burdens,
your hopes and regrets.
An invitation if you feel good today,
and an invitation if you do not,
if you are aching—
    and there are so many ways to ache.

Whoever you are, however you are,
wherever you are in your journey,
this is an invitation into peace.
    Peace in your heart,
    and peace in your heart,
    and—with every breath—
    peace in your heart.

Maybe your heart is heavy
or hardened.
Maybe it's troubled
and peace can take up residence
only in a small corner,
only on the edge,
with all that is going on in the world,
and in your life.
Ni modo. It doesn't matter.

All that you need
for a deep and comforting peace to grow
lies within you.
Once it is in your heart
let it spread into your life,
let it pour from your life into the world—
and once it is in the world,
let it shine upon all beings.

HOW POETS PRAY

What do you do with the secret verses of your heart? With your need for redemption, the story without words? With paradoxical truths, too private and nuanced to share, that cannot be printed or spoken aloud?

You weave their energy into a poem, carefully, carefully, over and under and through, luminescent strands that cannot be un-teased, until the poem is shot through with light from an unknown origin. And you whisper it into the dark. Breeze-forms delivered into the deep.

UNITARIAN UNIVERSALIST MEDITATION MANUALS

Unitarians and Universalists have been publishing prayer collections and meditation manuals for more than 170 years. In 1841 the Unitarians broke with their tradition of addressing only theological topics and published *Short Prayers for the Morning and Evening of Every Day in the Week, with Occasional Prayers and Thanksgivings*. Over the years, the Unitarians published many more volumes of prayers, including Theodore Parker's selections. In 1938 *Gaining a Radiant Faith* by Henry H. Saunderson launched the tradition of an annual Lenten manual.

Several Universalist collections appeared in the early nineteenth century. A comprehensive Book of Prayers was published in 1839, featuring both public and private devotions. Like the Unitarians, the Universalists published Lenten manuals, and in the 1950s they complemented this series with Advent manuals.

Since 1961, the year the Unitarians and Universalists consolidated, the Lenten manual has evolved into a meditation manual.

For a complete list of meditation manuals, please visit www.uua.org/skinner/meditation